4.1

T 18620

DUE

The Nez Perce Tribe

by Allison Lassieur

Consultants:
Josiah Pinkham, Ethnographer
Cultural Resource Program
Nez Perce Tribe

William R. Swagerty
Associate Professor of History
University of Idaho

Bridgestone Books
an imprint of Capstone Press
Mankato, Minnesota

Bridgestone Books are published by Capstone Press
151 Good Counsel Drive, P.O. Box 669, Mankato, Minnesota 56002
http://www.capstone-press.com

Library of Congress Cataloging-in-Publication Data
Lassieur, Allison.
    The Nez Perce Tribe/by Allison Lassieur.
        p. cm.—(Native peoples)
    Includes bibliographical references and index.
    Summary: An overview of the past and present lives of the Nez Perce tribe including
their history, homes, food, clothing, family life, customs, religion, and government.
        ISBN 0-7368-0500-1
        1. Nez Perce Indians—History—Juvenile literature. 2. Nez Perce Indians—Social life
and customs—Juvenile literature. [1. Nez Perce Indians. 2. Indians of North America—
Northwest, Pacific.] I. Title. II. Series.
E99.N5 L36 2000
979.5'0049741—dc21   99-053167

Editorial Credits
Rebecca Glaser, editor; Timothy Halldin, cover designer and illustrator; Kimberly Danger
    and Katy Kudela, photo researchers

Photo Credits
Corbis, 20
David Jensen, 8, 12
Department of the Interior/National Park Service/
    Nez Perce National Historic Park, 10
Marilyn "Angel" Wynn, cover, 18
Montana Historical Society, Helena, 6
Photo Network/Mark Newman, 16
Unicorn Stock Photos/Jeff Greenberg, 14

1 2 3 4 5 6 05 04 03 02 01 00

Table of Contents

Traditional Location

The Nez Perce people lived in the northwestern United States where Oregon, Washington, and Idaho meet. They also lived in what is now western Montana. The Clearwater, Salmon, Snake, Lochsa, Selway, Imnaha, and Grande Ronde rivers flow through the Nez Perce homeland. The tribe lives in the same areas today.

Fast Facts

Most Nez Perce people live on reservations today. Some live in cities. The Nez Perce live like many other North Americans. They are proud of their history and they keep their traditions. These facts tell about the history of the Nez Perce people.

Homes: Early Nez Perce lived in many kinds of houses. Some used dirt to build round pit houses with rounded roofs. Others built large longhouses covered with reed mats. Later, the Nez Perce made their homes from buffalo skin.

Food: The Nez Perce gathered roots, plants, berries, and nuts. Camas root was one of their main foods. The Nez Perce hunted many game animals such as buffalo. They fished for salmon, trout, and other fish.

Clothing: Nez Perce men wore buckskin shirts and leggings with fringe. Nez Perce women wore buckskin dresses that had fringe. They decorated their clothing with beads, shells, and elk teeth. Both men and women wore moccasins and buffalo-skin robes.

Language: The Nez Perce language is part of a group of languages called Sahaptian. Only native people in the northwestern United States speak Sahaptian languages.

Nez Perce History

The Nez Perce lived in permanent villages during winter. These camps were in low areas near rivers. During spring and summer, the Nez Perce traveled to higher lands to hunt, fish, and gather food.

In 1805, the Nez Perce met members of the Lewis and Clark expedition. The tribe made friends with these white explorers. The explorers were among the first white men to come to Nez Perce lands.

In 1877, the Nez Perce War began. The U.S. government wanted all the Nez Perce to live on small reservations. But the Nez Perce did not want to give up their land.

Chief Joseph and other leaders fled northeast toward Canada with 750 Nez Perce. The soldiers followed and attacked. More than 300 Nez Perce were killed. Chief Joseph was sad to see his people hurt and dying. When he surrendered, he said, "I will fight no more forever."

Chief Joseph led his people toward Canada to escape from U.S. soldiers.

The Nez Perce People

Nez Perce call themselves Nimiipuu (NEE-mee-poo). This word means "the real people." French fur traders called the Nimiipuu "Nez Perce." The name means pierced nose in French. Piercing noses was not a Nez Perce custom. But some Nez Perce may have borrowed the custom from other tribes.

The Nez Perce are known for their excellent skill with horses. The tribe is famous for breeding Appaloosas. These spotted horses are a symbol of Nez Perce life.

The Nez Perce are proud of their history. Children learn their traditional language. The Nez Perce work to preserve their history and culture.

Today, most Nez Perce live on reservations in the northwestern United States. They also live in cities around the world. Some tribal members have become successful in business. They all share a respect for their past life and culture.

The Nez Perce are famous for their horse-riding skills.

Homes, Food, and Clothing

In the past, Nez Perce built many kinds of homes. One was the kuhétini-t (koo-HAT-in-eet). The Nez Perce built these longhouses from wooden posts and reed mats. Longhouses looked short from the outside. The Nez Perce dug out the floors so there was plenty of room. The longhouses were warm.

The most common home was a walí-mini-t (wahl-LEE-min-eet). This type of house was cone-shaped and was covered with reed mats or buffalo skins.

The Nez Perce traveled seasonally to gather food. The men fished and hunted game such as elk, deer, and buffalo. Women picked berries, gathered nuts, and dug camas roots. The Nez Perce ate the bulbs of this blue flower. Women also prepared food.

Early Nez Perce wore clothes made from animal skins. Men wore shirts and leggings. Women wore dresses. Nez Perce began wearing clothes made from cloth when Europeans came to North America.

A walí-mini-t was the most common Nez Perce home. The cone-shaped houses could be moved easily.

The Nez Perce and Horses

Many Native American groups caught horses that ran away from Spanish explorers. The Nez Perce traded goods with these groups for horses. They used the horses to travel, hunt, trade, and fish.

The Nez Perce had the best horse skills in the Northwest. Almost everyone in a Nez Perce village owned a horse. People who owned many horses had more influence than people who owned fewer horses.

The Nez Perce made trappings for their horses. They made these fancy coverings from buckskins, horseskins, and cornhusks. They decorated trappings with paint, dye, and beads.

The Nez Perce used horses to carry supplies between winter and summer camps. The horses pulled a sepé-sepen (suh-PA-suh-pan). The Nez Perce made this sled from two wooden poles and animal skins. They carried as many supplies as they could on the sepé-sepen. They buried the rest of their supplies to save for when they returned to their camp.

The Nez Perce still make trappings for their horses today.

Nez Perce Families

Family life has always been important to the Nez Perce. Many members of a Nez Perce family lived together in a longhouse. Several families lived in one village.

The Nez Perce did not have a formal marriage ceremony. When a man and a woman wanted to get married, their families exchanged gifts. The gifts could be horses, food, baskets, or other items. After they were married, the man and woman lived with either the man's or the woman's family. They lived where they were needed most.

The Nez Perce kept babies in cradleboards until they could walk. Mothers wore cradleboards on their backs. Uncles and aunts helped raise children. Boys learned to hunt and fish. Girls learned to gather food and cook.

Grandparents taught their grandchildren stories about the Nez Perce. The stories taught Nez Perce history, traditions, beliefs, and values.

Families are an important part of Nez Perce life.

Creation Story

Nez Perce stories tell how different parts of nature were created. This story explains how the Nez Perce people began.

Coyote was alone. A monster had eaten all the other animals. Coyote decided to play a trick on the monster. Coyote cried, "Oh, Monster! You must eat me. I am lonely since you ate all the animals." So the monster ate Coyote in one huge bite.

Coyote had packed tools to hurt the monster. He set the monster's stomach on fire. He cut out the monster's heart with a knife.

Soon, the monster died. Coyote carved the monster's body and threw the pieces all over the world. Everywhere a piece fell, a new group of people came to life.

Coyote had forgotten to put people on the land where he stood. Coyote washed his paws and tossed the water on the ground. People appeared where the drops fell. They became the Nimiipuu.

After Coyote created the last group of people, he said, "You will be known as Nimiipuu." Nimiipuu means "the real people."

Nez Perce Religion

The Nez Perce think of Earth as a mother. They believe that all animals, plants, and land are related.

The Nez Perce believe that people receive spiritual power from their ancestors and the environment. The power sometimes comes in the form of visions. Nez Perce go on vision quests to find their vision. Songs also are important to the Nez Perce. A person sometimes finds his or her song during the vision quest. A person also may receive a guardian spirit called a wé-yekin (WAY-yah-kin).

The Nez Perce show their power and beliefs through dances. Today, the Nez Perce perform some of their traditional dances around the country. Other dances are private. Only members of the tribe or others who are invited may attend.

Some Nez Perce follow Christianity. This religion follows the teachings of Jesus Christ.

The Nez Perce perform some of their traditional dances around the country.

Nez Perce Government

In the past, each Nez Perce village had its own council. The council was made up of men selected from the village. The council members discussed problems and made laws.

The leader of the village council usually was the oldest man in the village. Some councils had a peace chief and a war chief. The peace chief took care of the village in times of peace. The war chief led men into battle.

Villages often came together to trade, to celebrate, and to defend themselves against enemies. The village members gathered under one leader. This leader usually was the most influential member of the group. Other important members of the villages helped the leader.

Today, the Nez Perce still have a tribal council. This group is called the Nez Perce Tribal Executive Committee. The council works to make life better for tribal members.

Chief Looking Glass was a famous Nez Perce chief who lived during the 1800s.

Hands On: Make an Isáaptakay

The Nez Perce made carrying pouches out of rawhide. This type of pouch was called an isáaptakay (i-SAHP-ti-kye). People carried dried foods and clothing in an isáaptakay while traveling. They decorated isáaptakays with colorful designs. You can make an isáaptakay from paper.

What You Need

A large sheet of heavy paper   Scissors
String   Hole punch
Crayons, paint, or markers

What You Do

1. Lay the sheet of heavy paper on a table. Fold the right edge to the middle. Then fold the left edge to the middle. The edges of the paper should meet in the center.
2. With the paper still folded, fold the top edge down and the bottom edge up. These edges also should meet in the middle. Now you have a pouch.
3. Punch one hole in each edge that is on the top of the pouch. Thread the string through the holes and tie it. This keeps your isáaptakay closed.
4. Untie and unfold your isáaptakay. Use crayons, paint, or markers to decorate it.

Words to Know

council (KOUN-suhl)—a group of leaders

isáaptakay (i-SAHP-ti-kye)—a carrying pouch made of rawhide

preserve (pree-ZURV)—to protect something so it stays in its original form

religion (ri-LIJ-uhn)—a set of spiritual beliefs people follow

sepé-sepen (suh-PA-suh-pan)—an object made from two wooden poles covered with animal skins; horses pull sepé-sepens.

surrender (suh-REN-dur)—to give up

symbol (SIM-buhl)—something that stands for something else

traditional (truh-DISH-uhn-uhl)—having to do with the ways of the past

Read More

Boulé, Mary Null. *Plateau Region: Nez Perce People.* Native Americans of North America. Vashon, Wash.: Merryant Publishers, 1998.

Hubbard-Brown, Janet. *Native American Leaders.* Costume, Tradition, and Culture. Philadelphia: Chelsea House Publishers, 1999.

McAuliffe, Bill. *Chief Joseph of the Nez Perce.* Photo-Illustrated Biographies. Mankato, Minn.: Bridgestone Books, 1998.

Useful Addresses

**Nez Perce National
  Historic Park**
Route 1, Box 100
Spalding, ID 83551

Nez Perce Tribe of Idaho
P.O. Box 365
Lapwai, ID 83540

Internet Sites

Nez Perce Education and Information
http://www.nezperce.com/npeindex.html
Nez Perce Indians
http://www.lewis-clarkvalley.com/indian.html
Nez Perce National Historical Museum Collection
http://www.uidaho.edu/nezperce/archmap.htm
Nez Perce/Nee-mee-poo Home page
http://www.uidaho.edu/nezperce/neemepoo.htm

Index